THE LESSONS IN THIS BOOK CORRELATE TO THE COMMON CORE STATE STANDARDS

COMMON CORE STATE STANDARDS

BARKER CREEK

Prefixes & Suffixes

Text and Illustration
Copyright © 2014
by Barker Creek Publishing, Inc.

Graphic Designer: Vickie Spurgin

Printed in the USA

ISBN: 978-1-928961-56-7
Item Number: LL-1606

BARKER CREEK®
P.O. Box 2610
Poulsbo, WA 98730
www.barkercreek.com
800.692.5833

Prefixes & Activity Book

A Reading FUNdamentals™ Book

M000019131

Other books in this series include:
Homonyms, Synonyms & Antonyms Activity Book
Compound Words Activity Book
Nouns Activity Book
Verbs & Adverbs Activity Book
Adjectives Activity Book
Collective Nouns Activity Book
Idioms Activity Book
Similes Activity Book

Chart Sets in this series include:
Homonyms, Synonyms & Antonyms Chart Set
Compound Words Chart Set
Noun Chart Set
Verbs & Adverb Chart Set
Adjectives Chart Set
Collective Nouns Chart Set
Prefixes/Suffixes Chart Set
Idioms Chart Set
Similes Chart Set

All of the titles in our
Reading FUNdamentals™ series
are also available as E-Books.

Visit us at www.barkercreek.com
for more information.

Prefix

a letter or letters that are added to the beginning of a word to form a new word

○ **tele-**: *distant*
telephone • teleport • telescope • television

○ **re-**: *again*
recycle • recreate • review • replace

○ **in-, im-, il-, ir-**: *not*
invisible • impossible • illegible • irreplaceable

○ **multi-**: *many*
multilingual • multiply • multifunction • multipurpose

Suffix

a letter or letters that are added to the end of a word to form a new word

○ **-ward**: *towards*
backward • forward • homeward • inward

○ **-able**: *can be (done)*
likeable • affordable • noticeable • portable

○ **-ology**: *study of*
biology • geology • technology • zoology

○ **-ly**: *like, characteristic of*
daily • totally • quickly • accurately

Table of Contents

Ideas/How to Use This Book 4

Answer Key 5-6

What is a Prefix? 7

   bi- 8

   cent- 9

   cir- 10

   ex- 11

   hydr- 12

   inter- 13

   mono- 14

   multi- 15

   oct- 16

   re- 17

   semi- 18

   sub- 19

   super- 20

   tele- 21

   tri- 22

   uni- 23

What is a Suffix? 24

   -age 25

   -al 26

   -ary 27

   -er 28

   -able 29

   -ful 30

   -hood 31

   -ic 32

   -ist 33

   -less 34

   -ling 35

   -or 36

   -ous 37

   -ship 38

   -tion 39

   -y 40

Prefix Template 41

Suffix Template 42

Prefix/Suffix Word Pictures . . . 43-46

Prefix Review Test 47

Suffix Review Test 48

More Prefixes 49

More Suffixes 50

How to Use This Book

Please read through this entire page before getting started.

This book contains 32 lessons for teaching prefixes and suffixes. These can be studied throughout the year or when you are specifically discussing prefixes and suffixes. This book also introduces many NEW VOCABULARY WORDS.

Page Set Up

*(**NOTE**: At the top of the page you will see a wrench. Inside the wrench is a specific prefix or suffix with its meaning. This will indicate what the lesson covers.)*

1. Create a blueprint!
Draw it! The student will **add details** to show the meaning of the sentence located at the bottom of the blueprint area. The sentence includes the specific word being discussed.

2. Survey it!
Look it up! Using a dictionary, the student will look up the specific word and write its meaning in the space provided.

3. Saw through it!
Read each of the four prefix or suffix related words. Next to each word is its meaning. Read through the four meanings.

4. Put on your hard hat!
Think about it! Read the four sentences and decide which of the four vocabulary words best completes each sentence. Write the word in the blank. (Encourage the students to use the process of elimination.) There may be other words in the sentence that they do not know, so this process comes in handy!

5. Tack it on!
Turn the paper to the side, and you will see this **EXTRA** activity. These activities range from websites to visit, hands-on activities, critical thinking activities and more! These can be used as a home activity.

Blank Page Templates

There are two blank templates provided on pages 41 and 42. These are for you to choose other prefixes and suffixes not used in this book.

Picture Cards

There are 32 prefix and suffix REPRODUCIBLE pictures found on pages 43-46 . These are the same illustrations found on the lesson pages.
Here are some ideas for using the pictures:

Vocabulary
Use the pictures for a matching activity. Have each of the vocabulary words written on an index card for matching the pictures to their correct words. Write the prefixes and suffixes within each word in red so the students can identify them.
*(**NOTE**: The pictures are in the same order as the pages in the book.)*

Flip Books
AFTER each lesson, give each student the illustration to color and label the prefix or suffix on the back. Punch a hole and add yarn for a little book to take home.

Prefix/Suffix Extensions
Upon completing the book, allow the students to randomly choose a picture. Have them color the picture and glue to the top of a white piece of paper. Then have the students name the picture, identify the prefix or suffix, and find 5-10 more words that begin or end the same. A dictionary is helpful! Write these words and draw a picture for each, showing the meaning of the words.

Review Tests

Measure what your students have learned. See the tests on pages 47-48. One test is a review of prefixes and the other test is a review of suffixes.

More Prefixes and More Suffixes

On pages 49-50 you will find a list of other prefixes and suffixes that are not highlighted in this book. These may be reproduced and given to the students for more related activities.

Answer Key

The answers for each of the lessons can be found on pages 5-6. You will also find the answers to the review tests.

ANSWER KEY

Page 8
1. bilingual
2. bicycle
3. bicuspid
4. bicep

Page 9
1. centimeter
2. cent
3. century
4. centennial

Page 10
1. circumference
2. circumstance
3. circulate
4. circular

Page 11
1. explore
2. example
3. exit
4. exhale

Page 12
1. hydroelectric
2. hydrogen
3. hydroplane
4. hydrophobia

Page 13
1. interior
2. interview
3. intermediate
4. international

Page 14
1. monotone
2. monochromic
3. monorail
4. monopoly

Page 15
1. multicolor
2. multiple
3. multivitamin
4. multipurpose

Page 16
1. octet
2. octagon
3. octane
4. October

Page 17
1. repair
2. rehearse
3. respect
4. reside

Page 18
1. semitransparent
2. semifinal
3. semiannual
4. semicolon

Page 19
1. subway
2. submerge
3. subsoil
4. subside

Page 20
1. superb
2. superior
3. superhuman
4. superintendent

Page 21
1. television
2. telephoto
3. telephone
4. telegraph

Page 22
1. tricycle
2. trilogy
3. triathlon
4. trident

Page 23
1. unicorn
2. uniform
3. unique
4. universe

Page 25
1. shortage
2. storage
3. courage
4. carriage

Page 26
1. decimal
2. seasonal
3. tropical
4. natural

Page 27
1. sanctuary
2. library
3. stationary
4. estuary

Page 28
1. speaker
2. astronomer
3. teacher
4. lawyer

Page 29
1. comfortable
2. honorable
3. likeable
4. favorable

Page 30
1. thoughtful
2. skillful
3. bountiful
4. faithful

Page 31
1. childhood
2. brotherhood
3. statehood
4. motherhood

Page 32
1. volcanic
2. rustic
3. patriotic
4. heroic

Page 33

1. dentist
2. pianist
3. ventriloquist
4. artist

Page 34

1. careless
2. helpless
3. timeless
4. scoreless

Page 35

1. inkling
2. darling
3. sapling
4. fledgling

Page 36

1. emperor
2. tailor
3. ancestor
4. juror

Page 37

1. famous
2. gracious
3. industrious
4. virtuous

Page 38

1. hardship
2. citizenship
3. fellowship
4. championship

Page 39

1. opposition
2. vacation
3. participation
4. tradition

Page 40

1. furry
2. sleepy
3. wealthy
4. whimsy

PREFIX REVIEW TEST — Page 47

1. bicep
2. recycle
3. telescope
4. semicircle
5. century
6. circumference

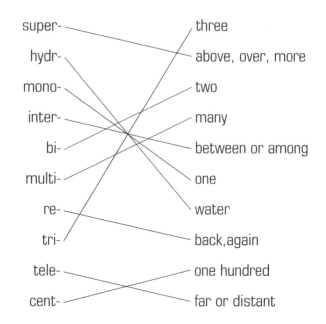

super-   three
hydr-   above, over, more
mono-   two
inter-   many
bi-   between or among
multi-   one
re-   water
tri-   back, again
tele-   one hundred
cent-   far or distant

bi,   uni,   inter,   mono,   multi

SUFFIX REVIEW TEST — Page 48

1. famous
2. shortage
3. dirty
4. sapling
5. duckling
6. participation

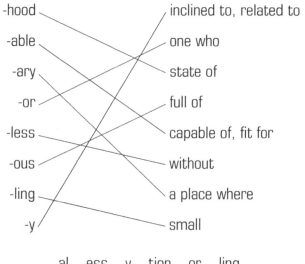

-hood   inclined to, related to
-able   one who
-ary   state of
-or   full of
-less   capable of, fit for
-ous   without
-ling   a place where
-y   small

al,   ess,   y,   tion,   or,   ling

What is a prefix?

a syllable added to the **beginning** of a word to change the meaning of the word

Name: _____

bi | two

 **bi** focals

Create a blueprint!

Draw it!

Add details to the illustration to show the meaning of the sentence.

Granny Pat wore her **bifocals** while reading the newspaper.

Survey it!

Look it up! Using a dictionary, write the definition of the word.

bi focals – _____

_____

Saw through it!

Read each of the four words and their definitions.

bicycle — *a wheeled vehicle that has two wheels and is moved by foot pedals*

bicep — *a muscle with two heads or points of origin*

bilingual — *a person who uses or is able to use two languages*

bicuspid — *having two points, as the crescent moon*

Put on your hard hat!

Think about it!

Use the four vocabulary words above to complete these sentences.

① Juan learned a new language and became _____.

② Nathan rides his _____ to school every day.

③ The dentist showed me the _____ that he pulled.

④ He lifts weights to strengthen his _____.

Create a large pair of glasses of out posterboard. Don't forget the space for your nose and the earpieces. Colored plastic wrap makes neat lenses.

Tack it on!

Name: _____

cent | one hundred

cent ipede

Create a blueprint!

Draw it!
Add details to the illustration to show the meaning of the sentence.

Survey it!

Look it up!
Using a dictionary, write the definition of the word.

Crawling out from under a pile of leaves was a **centipede**.

centipede – _____

_____

Saw through it!

Read each of the four words and their definitions.

centennial	*occurring <u>once</u> every 100 years*
century	*a period of 100 years*
centimeter	*a unit of length equal to one hundredth of a meter*
cent	*a coin worth one-hundredth of the value of the basic unit*

Put on your hard hat!

Think about it!

Use the four vocabulary words above to complete these sentences.

① The crumb measured only one _____,

② A penny is worth one _____.

③ A _____ ago, my great grandmother lived in this house.

④ The United States celebrated its _____ birthday in 1876.

Visit the website **www.enchantedlearning.com** and search centipede to learn more about this interesting critter.

Tack it on!

Name: _____

cir | around

circus

Create a blueprint!

Draw it!
Add details to the illustration to show the meaning of the sentence.

A banner sign, reading "The Greatest Show On Earth", hung above the **circus** tent.

Survey it!

Look it up!
Using a dictionary, write the definition of the word.

circus – _____

_____

Saw through it!

Read each of the four words and their definitions.

circular	*having the form of a circle*
circumference	*the boundary line of a circle*
circumstance	*a condition or fact that must be considered in determining a course of action*
circulate	*to move around in a course*

Put on your hard hat!

Think about it!
Use the four vocabulary words above to complete these sentences.

① Measure the _____ of the round table.

② Under no _____ am I allowed to answer the door for a stranger.

③ The heart's job is to _____ blood through the body.

④ We rode our bikes around the track in a _____ motion.

Imagine you are the circus ringmaster. Write a script you would perform announcing the circus to a large audience.

Tack it on!

Name: _____

ex | out of, outside

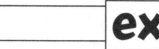 **ex** tinct

Create a blueprint!

Draw it!
Add details to the illustration to show the meaning of the sentence.

Drawings of the **extinct** dinosaurs made the pages of the book come alive.

Survey it!

Look it up!
Using a dictionary, write the definition of the word.

extinct _____

_____

Saw through it!

Read each of the four words and their definitions.

example — *one that is representative of a group as a whole*

exhale — *to breathe out*

exit — *the act of going away or out*

explore — *to search into or travel for the purpose of discovery*

Put on your hard hat!

Think about it!
Use the four vocabulary words above to complete these sentences.

 Scientists can _____ many things using a microscope.

 My paper was chosen as an _____ for others to follow.

 _____ the theater through these doors.

 The doctor wanted me to inhale and then _____.

Investigate and write five interesting facts about your favorite dinosaur. Create a diorama depicting its prehistoric environment.

Tack it on!

Name: _____

| hydr | water |

hydr ant

Create a blueprint!

Draw it!
Add details to the illustration to show the meaning of the sentence.

Survey it!

Look it up!
Using a dictionary, write the definition of the word.

Water squirted from the wriggling hose attached to the fire **hydrant**.

hydrant – _____

_____

Saw through it!

Read each of the four words and their definitions.

hydroplane   *a speedboat whose hull is raised as it glides over water*

hydrogen   *an element in chemistry that is colorless, odorless, and most abundant in the universe*

hydroelectric   *used in the production of electricity by water power*

hydrophobia   *an abnormal fear of water*

Put on your hard hat!

Think about it!

Use the four vocabulary words above to complete these sentences.

 ① The new dam provides _____ power.

 ② _____ is one of the elements in water.

 ③ The lake is full of _____ boats for the race.

 ④ Tim suffers from _____ every time we ride our bikes near the lake.

Check out **www.cpws.com** and click on Kids Pages for a fun puzzle of water words. Also read the informative water-saving tips.

Tack it on!

Name: _____

inter | between or among

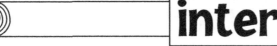

inter state

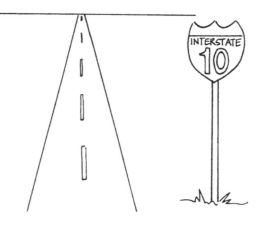

Create a blueprint!

Draw it!
Add details to the illustration to show the meaning of the sentence.

Interstate 10 leads directly to the large, metropolitan cityscape.

Survey it!

Look it up!
Using a dictionary, write the definition of the word.

interstate – _____

_____

Saw through it!

Read each of the four words and their definitions.

interior	*located on the inside; inner*
intermediate	*being or occurring in the middle or between*
international	*involving two or more nations*
interview	*a formal meeting in person, especially one arranged for the review of the qualifications of an applicant*

Put on your hard hat!

Think about it!

Use the four vocabulary words above to complete these sentences.

 The _____ of the car was dirty.

 Reporters _____ many people.

 The gymnast progressed from beginner to _____ level.

 The U.S. and Russia made an _____ agreement.

Pick a destination on a U.S. map that you have always wanted to visit. Use a ruler, map scale and legend to help you estimate how many miles away the destination is and how long it would take you to travel there.

Tack it on!

Reading FUNdamentals™
Prefixes

Name: _____

mono	one

mono cle

Along with the **monocle** and top hat, a bow tie and jacket completed George's costume for the school play.

monocle – _____

_____

Create a blueprint!

Draw it!

Add details to the illustration to show the meaning of the sentence.

Survey it!

Look it up!

Using a dictionary, write the definition of the word.

Saw through it!

Read each of the four words and their definitions.

monopoly	a company or group having exclusive control over a commercial activity
monorail	a railway system using a single rail
monotone	a succession of sounds or words uttered in a single tone of voice
monochromic	a picture, especially a painting, done in different shades of a single color

Put on your hard hat!

Think about it!

Use the four vocabulary words above to complete these sentences.

 Cheryl spoke in a _____ voice.

 The picture was _____ in color.

 We rode the _____ to the big city.

 The large company has a _____ in the industry.

Have you ever needed a costume for a play, event or holiday? Write a paragraph describing the costume.

Tack it on!

Reading FUNdamentals™ — Prefixes & Suffixes ©2014 Barker Creek Publishing, Inc. • www.barkercreek.com

Name: _____

| multi | many |

multiplication

Create a blueprint!

Draw it!
Add details to the illustration to show the meaning of the sentence.

Hannah was working her fifth **multiplication** problem on the blackboard.

Survey it!

Look it up!
Using a dictionary, write the definition of the word.

multiplication – _____

_____

Saw through it!

Read each of the four words and their definitions.

multipurpose	*designed or used for several purposes*
multivitamin	*containing many vitamins*
multicolor	*having many colors*
multiple	*consisting of more than one individual, element, part, or other component*

Put on your hard hat!

Think about it!

Use the four vocabulary words above to complete these sentences.

 The _____ rainbow was brilliant in the evening sky.

 There were _____ reasons why the children were so loud.

③ Remember to take a _____ to maintain good health.

 A paper plate can be used for eating or for various arts and crafts activities. It is a _____ item.

What is the common occurrence when you multiply a number by 10? 11?

Tack it on!

Name: _____

| oct | eight |

OCTopus

Swimming near the **octopus** was a large school of fish.

octopus – _____

_____

octagon	*a polygon with eight sides and eight angles*
octane	*a formula using elements in chemistry that is found in petroleum and used as fuel and solvent*
octet	*a composition for eight voices or eight instruments*
October	*the tenth month of the year (Special Note: October in latin means eight. October was the eighth month.)*

① We heard the _____ sing in harmony.

② The shape of the sign was an _____.

③ The fuel contained_____.

④ My birthday is in _____.

Here's a sea-purb dinner idea! Cut a hot dog in half long ways, leaving about an inch uncut. Cut each half into four strips per side (eight legs). Drop in boiling water for four minutes and add mustard eyes.

Tack it on!

Name: _____

 re | back, again

 recycle

Create
a blueprint!

Draw it!
Add details to
the illustration
to show the
meaning of
the sentence.

RECYCLE

Survey it!

Look it up!
Using a
dictionary, write
the definition
of the word.

The large truck stopped to pick up the full **recycle** bin.

recycle – _____

_____

Saw through it!

Read each of the
four words and
their definitions.

repair   *to renew or fix*

reside   *to live permanently and continuously dwell*

respect   *to feel or show polite regards for; esteem*

rehearse   *to practice in preparation for a public performance*

**Put on your
hard hat!**

Think about it!

Use the four
vocabulary
words above to
complete these
sentences.

① The plumber will _____ the broken faucet.

② The dance company will _____ the dance on stage.

③ Showing _____ will make your parents proud.

④ Carly and her family _____ in Dallas, Texas.

Interested in taking better care of our resources?
Visit **www.epa.gov/students** for some great information
and tips.

Tack
it on!

Name: _____

| semi | half |

semi-circle

Create a blueprint!

Draw it!

Add details to the illustration to show the meaning of the sentence.

Butterflies and bees were buzzing around the tulips, planted in a **semi-circle** pattern.

Survey it!

Look it up!

Using a dictionary, write the definition of the word.

semi-circle – _____

_____

Saw through it!

Read each of the four words and their definitions.

semi-colon	*a punctuation mark (;) used to connect independent clauses*
semifinal	*a match, competition, or examination that precedes the final one*
semiannual	*occurring or issued twice a year*
semitransparent	*partially transparent*

Put on your hard hat!

Think about it!

Use the four vocabulary words above to complete these sentences.

① The glass in the window was _____.

② In the tournament, we played in the _____ game.

③ My mother and I always go to the _____ sale at the mall.

④ When writing my report, I forgot to use a _____ in my final paragraph.

Two semi-circles joined together create a circle. Draw your own perfect circle with a compass. Draw a line down the middle to form two semi-circles.

Tack it on!

Name: _____

○ **sub** | under; beneath; below

submarine

Create a blueprint!

Draw it!
Add details to the illustration to show the meaning of the sentence.

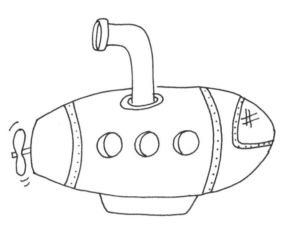

As I was scuba diving, I saw a **submarine**.

Survey it!

Look it up!
Using a dictionary, write the definition of the word.

submarine – _____

_____

Saw through it!

Read each of the four words and their definitions.

submerge	*to put under or plunge into water*
subsoil	*a layer of soil lying just under the topsoil*
subway	*an underground tunnel*
subside	*to become lower, sink*

Put on your hard hat!

Think about it!
Use the four vocabulary words above to complete these sentences.

① I took the _____ home today.

② The diver will _____ in the water.

③ The _____ is full of nutrients for the tomato plants.

④ The flooding waters did _____.

Create a submarine using recycled items. Afterwards, list the recycled items you used.

Tack it on!

Name: _____

super | above, over, more

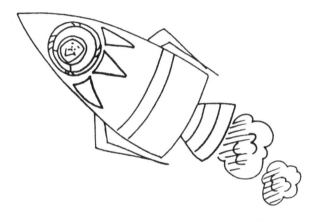

super sonic

At **supersonic** speed, the rocket flew around the universe.

supersonic – _____

_____

Create a blueprint!

Draw it!
Add details to the illustration to show the meaning of the sentence.

Survey it!

Look it up!
Using a dictionary, write the definition of the word.

Saw through it!

Read each of the four words and their definitions.

superhuman	beyond ordinary or normal human ability, power, or experience
superb	of unusually high quality; excellent
superior	higher than another in rank, station, or authority
superintendent	a person who has the authority to supervise or direct

Put on your hard hat!

Think about it!

Use the four vocabulary words above to complete these sentences.

① The dinner was _____!

② He needed to ask his _____ for permission.

③ The main character in this adventurous story had

_____ abilities.

④ The building _____ gave us a key to get in the door.

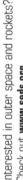

Interested in outer space and rockets?
Check out **www.seds.org**.

Tack it on!

Name: _____

tele | far or distance

tele scope

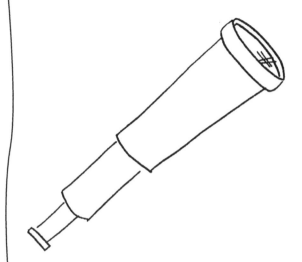

The **telescope** focused on a large star in the night sky.

Create a blueprint!

Draw it!
Add details to the illustration to show the meaning of the sentence.

Survey it!

Look it up!
Using a dictionary, write the definition of the word.

tele scope – _____

_____

Saw through it!

Read each of the four words and their definitions.

tele phone — *electronic equipment that allows people to communicate over distances*

tele vision — *broadcasting visual images of stationary or moving objects*

tele graph — *a device used to communicate at a distance over a wire*

tele photo — *a photographic lens or lens system used to produce a large image of a distant object*

Put on your hard hat!

Think about it!
Use the four vocabulary words above to complete these sentences.

① I like watching my favorite shows on the _____.

② The astronomer used a _____ lens to see the stars.

③ Use good manners when answering the _____.

④ The news from overseas was received by _____.

Tack it on!

Name: _____

tri | three

tri plets

Create a blueprint!

Draw it!
Add details to the illustration to show the meaning of the sentence.

Survey it!

Look it up!
Using a dictionary, write the definition of the word.

Each of the three **triplets** has a bottle that matches the color of her bonnet.

triplets – _____

_____

Saw through it!

Read each of the four words and their definitions.

triathlon — *athletic contests in which participants compete without stopping in three successive events, usually long-distance swimming, bicycling, and running*

tricycle — *a vehicle that has three wheels, one in front and two in back*

trilogy — *a group of three literary works related in subject or theme*

trident — *a long, three-pronged fork or weapon, especially a three-pronged spear used for fishing*

Put on your hard hat!

Think about it!
Use the four vocabulary words above to complete these sentences.

① My little brother likes to ride his blue _____.

② The author was famous for the _____ he wrote.

③ To participate in a _____, you need to be in great physical shape.

④ In the movie, the king had a magical _____ that caught hundreds of fish.

Now that you know the meaning of the prefix, **tri-** do you know why a triangle is called a **tri**angle? What is the difference between a *scalene, isosceles* and *equilateral* triangle?

Tack it on!

Name: _____

| uni | one |

uni cycle

Create a blueprint!

Draw it!
Add details to the illustration to show the meaning of the sentence.

Carrying a striped umbrella, the clown rode the **unicycle** around the circus ring.

Survey it!

Look it up!
Using a dictionary, write the definition of the word.

unicycle – _____

_____

Saw through it!

Read each of the four words and their definitions.

uniform   *always the same*

unique   *being the only one of its kind*

universe   *all created things viewed as one system or a whole*

unicorn   *an imaginary creature represented as a white horse with a long horn growing from its forehead*

Put on your hard hat!

Think about it!
Use the four vocabulary words above to complete these sentences.

1. Harold won a stuffed _____ at the carnival.

2. The nurse wore a _____ when she worked at the hospital.

3. We all have a _____ thumbprint.

4. The _____ contains all the planets and stars.

Have you ever tried to juggle? Grab 3 small, soft balls and give it a try!

Tack it on!

What is a suffix?

a syllable added to the **end** of a word to change the meaning of the word

Name: _____

| age | state of |

marri**age**

Create a blueprint!

Draw it!
Add details to the illustration to show the meaning of the sentence.

Survey it!

Look it up!
Using a dictionary, write the definition of the word.

Standing under a palm tree, the couple enjoyed the sunset while celebrating twenty years of **marriage**.

marri**age** – _____

_____

Saw through it!

Read each of the four words and their definitions.

cour**age** — *the state or quality of mind or spirit that enables one to face danger or fear with composure, confidence, and resolution; bravery*

stor**age** — *a space for storing goods*

short**age** — *a deficiency in amount; an insufficiency*

carri**age** — *a wheeled support or frame for carrying a heavy object*

Put on your hard hat!

Think about it!

Use the four vocabulary words above to complete these sentences.

① There was a _____ of gas in the 1980s.

② We put all of the boxes in _____ for safe-keeping.

③ It took _____ to tell the truth.

④ We enjoyed a _____ ride through the country.

Interview a grandparent or elderly family friend who has been married for many years. Ask them to tell you about the time they first met their spouse.

Tack it on!

Name: _____

al | like, pertaining to

music **al**

John is very **musical** and plays several instruments.

music**al** – _____

_____

natur**al**	*not altered, treated, or disguised*
season**al**	*of or dependent on a particular season*
tropic**al**	*of, occurring in, or characteristic of the tropics*
decim**al**	*a number written using the base 10*

 "What is a _____ ?" my math teacher asked.

 Football is a _____ sport.

 We are going on a _____ vacation in Jamaica.

 Her _____ abilities make her a good ballerina.

Create a "guitar" using an empty tissue box, paper tube and rubber bands.

Tack it on!

Name: _____

| **ary** | a place where |

diction**ary**

Create a blueprint!

Draw it!
Add details to the illustration to show the meaning of the sentence.

Professor Quimby has a large **dictionary**, a pen, three paperclips and a ring of keys sitting on his desk.

Survey it!

Look it up!
Using a dictionary, write the definition of the word.

diction**ary** – _____

_____

Saw through it!

Read each of the four words and their definitions.

libr**ary**	a place in which literary and artistic materials, such as books, newspapers, pamphlets, prints, records, and tapes, are kept for reading or lending
sanctu**ary**	a sacred place, such as a church, temple, or mosque
estu**ary**	an arm of the sea that extends inland to meet the mouth of a river
station**ary**	not capable of being moved

Put on your hard hat!

Think about it!
Use the four vocabulary words above to complete these sentences.

① The meeting was held in the church's _____.

② I checked out many books at the _____.

③ We remained _____ while the President's car drove by.

④ The water is cold in the _____.

Flip through the dictionary and find an unfamiliar word. Read the definition and use the word in conversation three times today. Try it everyday for a week!

Tack it on!

Name: _____

er | one who

bak **er**

Create a blueprint!

Draw it!
Add details to the illustration to show the meaning of the sentence.

Survey it!

Look it up!
Using a dictionary, write the definition of the word.

Hallie the **baker** created a beautiful three tiered birthday cake.

bak**er** – _____

_____

Saw through it!

Read each of the four words and their definitions.

astronom**er**	one who specializes in astronomy, the science of studying stars
teach**er**	one who teaches, especially one hired to teach
lawy**er**	one whose profession is to give legal advice and assistance to clients and represent them in court or in other legal matters
speak**er**	one who delivers a public speech

Put on your hard hat!

Think about it!

Use the four vocabulary words above to complete these sentences.

① The class listened to the _____ as he told his story.

② We met an _____ when we visited NASA.

③ Our _____ did not give us any homework tonight.

④ My uncle went to law school to become a _____.

Create a recipe for your favorite dessert. Include ingredients, mixing and baking information.

Tack it on!

Suffixes

Name: _____

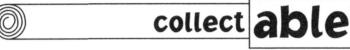

able | capable of, fit for

collect**able**

Create a blueprint!

Draw it!
Add details to the illustration to show the meaning of the sentence.

The actor was told her costume is very **collectable**.

Survey it!

Look it up!
Using a dictionary, write the definition of the word.

collect**able** – _____

_____

Saw through it!

Read each of the four words and their definitions.

comfort**able**   *feeling relaxed*

favor**able**   *something that is deemed advantageous or having a benefit*

honor**able**   *worthy of respect*

like**able**   *readily or easily liked*

Put on your hard hat!

Think about it!

Use the four vocabulary words above to complete these sentences.

① We want a _____ chair for our living room.

② Her courage was very _____ .

③ Our new teacher is very _____ .

④ I have a very _____ feeling that today is going to be a great day!

Design a fantasy castle fit for a prince or princess.

Tack it on!

Name: _____

 **ful** | full of

color **ful**

Create a blueprint!

Draw it!
Add details to the illustration to show the meaning of the sentence.

Shining through the gray sky and rain-filled clouds was a **colorful** rainbow.

Survey it!

Look it up!
Using a dictionary, write the definition of the word.

colorful – _____

_____

Saw through it!

Read each of the four words and their definitions.

bounti**ful**	*giving freely and generously; liberal*
faith**ful**	*reliable, firm in devoting or support*
skill**ful**	*possessing or exercising skill; expert*
thought**ful**	*engrossed in thought; contemplative*

Put on your hard hat!

Think about it!

Use the four vocabulary words above to complete these sentences.

① Sending a card to someone is very _____.

② The surgeon was _____ during surgery.

③ At Thanksgiving, food is _____ at grandma's house.

④ Susan is a _____ employee. She never misses work.

Experiment with color mixing using food coloring. Fill a glass half full with water and add a few drops of coloring. Drop in another color and stir. What happens?

Tack it on!

Name: _____

hood | state of

neighbor **hood**

Create a blueprint!

Draw it!
Add details to the illustration to show the meaning of the sentence.

Large trees created a canopy over the **neighborhood** houses.

Survey it!

Look it up!
Using a dictionary, write the definition of the word.

neighbor**hood** – _____

_____

Saw through it!

Read each of the four words and their definitions.

brother**hood**	an association of men united for common purposes
mother**hood**	the state of being a mother
child**hood**	the early stage in the existence or development of something
state**hood**	the status of being a state, especially of the United States, rather than being a territory or dependency

Put on your hard hat!

Think about it!
Use the four vocabulary words above to complete these sentences.

① During most of my _____, I lived in Arkansas.

② Daniel was proud of the _____ he shared with the other boys in his scout troop.

③ Texas achieved _____ in 1845.

④ _____ is a rewarding experience.

Draw a map from your house to a favorite local destination. Under the picture, write directions to the location.

Tack it on!

Name: _____

ic | like

artist **ic**

Create a blueprint!

Draw it!
Add details to the illustration to show the meaning of the sentence.

The **artistic** student painted a unique mural on the wall.

Survey it!

Look it up!
Using a dictionary, write the definition of the word.

artist**ic** – _____

_____

Saw through it!

Read each of the four words and their definitions.

hero**ic**	*having, displaying, or characteristic of the qualities appropriate to a hero; courageous*
volcan**ic**	*caused by a volcano or volcanoes*
patriot**ic**	*feeling, expressing, or inspired by love for one's country*
rust**ic**	*typical of country life or country people*

Put on your hard hat!

Think about it!
Use the four vocabulary words above to complete these sentences.

1. We saw a _____ explosion in Hawaii.

2. Our family stayed in a log cabin near the lake. It was very _____.

3. We felt _____ when we heard the *National Anthem* play.

4. John saved a boy from drowning. He was _____.

Research the artist Pablo Picasso and check out the website **www.picassohead.com**.

Tack it on!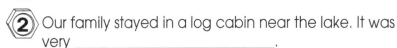

Name: _____

ist | one who

scient **ist**

Create a blueprint!

Draw it!
Add details to the illustration to show the meaning of the sentence.

Blue, fizzy potion bubbled and overflowed from the **scientist's** beaker, creating a huge mess!

Survey it!

Look it up!
Using a dictionary, write the definition of the word.

scient**ist** – _____

_____

Saw through it!

Read each of the four words and their definitions.

art**ist**	*a person who does creative work with sensitivity and imagination*
dent**ist**	*a person who is trained and licensed to practice dentistry*
pian**ist**	*a person who plays the piano*
ventriloqu**ist**	*a performer who projects their voice into a wooden dummy*

Put on your hard hat!

Think about it!

Use the four vocabulary words above to complete these sentences.

① I have an appointment today with the _____ to get my teeth cleaned.

② The music heard in the hotel was being played by a

_____.

③ The _____ used several voices during his skit.

④ The _____ used a unique painting technique.

Create your own fizzy potion at home! In the kitchen sink, pour a small mound of baking soda. Add some vinegar to the mound and watch it fizz!

Tack it on!

Name: _____

less | without

tire**less**

Heading for the finish line, the **tireless** runner won the race.

tire**less** – _____

_____

care**less**   *taking insufficient care; negligent*

help**less**   *unable to help oneself; powerless or incompetent*

score**less**   *having no points scored*

time**less**   *independent of time; eternal*

① Helen was _____ and poured too much juice.

② The little old lady seemed _____ trying to carry the heavy groceries.

③ This photograph is _____!

④ The hockey game was _____ at the end of the second period.

Suffixes

Name: _____

ling | small

duck **ling**

Create a blueprint!

Draw it!
Add details to the illustration to show the meaning of the sentence.

Splashing around in the water puddles was a cute yellow **duckling**.

Survey it!

Look it up!
Using a dictionary, write the definition of the word.

duck**ling** – _____

_____

Saw through it!

Read each of the four words and their definitions.

dar**ling**   *one that is greatly liked or preferred; a favorite*

fledg**ling**   *a young bird*

sap**ling**   *a young tree*

ink**ling**   *a slight understanding or vague idea or notion*

Put on your hard hat!

Think about it!
Use the four vocabulary words above to complete these sentences.

① I had an _____ that she would win the contest.

② My dad calls my mom _____ all the time.

③ The leaves fell off of the _____.

④ The _____ fell from his nest.

Make a list of seven more baby animals: (example: kid–baby goat)

Tack it on!

Name: _____

| **or** | one who |

sail **or**

Create a blueprint!

Draw it!
Add details to the illustration to show the meaning of the sentence.

Dan dreamed of being a **sailor**, cruising on a large ship in the deep, blue ocean.

Survey it!

Look it up!
Using a dictionary, write the definition of the word.

sail**or** – _____

_____

Saw through it!

Read each of the four words and their definitions.

jur**or**	one who serves as a member of a jury
ancest**or**	a person from whom one is descended, especially if more remote than a grandparent
emper**or**	the male ruler of an empire
tail**or**	one that makes, repairs, and alters garments such as suits, coats, and dresses

Put on your hard hat!

Think about it!
Use the four vocabulary words above to complete these sentences.

1. In the story, the _____ ruled for a very short time.

2. The pants need to be hemmed by a _____.

3. I learned that Daniel Boone was an _____ on my father's side of the family.

4. The _____ did not believe the defendant's testimony.

Visit the website: **http://boyslife.org/video-audio/644/learn-to-tie-knots**. Use a piece of rope and see if you can tie any of the knots shown.

Tack it on!

Name: _____

| OUS | full of |

studi **OUS**

Create a blueprint!

Draw it!

Add details to the illustration to show the meaning of the sentence.

Larry is very **studious** and works tirelessly on his homework.

Survey it!

Look it up!

Using a dictionary, write the definition of the word.

studi**ous** – _____

_____

Saw through it!

Read each of the four words and their definitions.

fam**ous**   *well or widely known*

graci**ous**   *characterized by kindness and warm courtesy*

industri**ous**   *skillful; clever*

virtu**ous**   *having or showing virtue, especially moral excellence*

Put on your hard hat!

Think about it!

Use the four vocabulary words above to complete these sentences.

① Cameron became _____ after writing an award-winning book.

② She was very _____ when she received the trophy.

③ The boys were _____ when they built a tall tower using small wooden blocks.

④ The star citizen of the week has _____ qualities.

List five subjects you study in school. Arrange the list into three different lists: 1) alphabetical 2) favorite to least favorite 3) shortest word to longest word.

Tack it on!

Name: _____

ship | state of

friend**ship**

Create a blueprint!

Draw it!
Add details to the illustration to show the meaning of the sentence.

Ellie and Elizabeth wore matching bracelets, celebrating their **friendship**.

Survey it!

Look it up!
Using a dictionary, write the definition of the word.

friend**ship** – _____

_____

Saw through it!

Read each of the four words and their definitions.

citizen**ship**	*the status of a citizen with its attendant duties, rights, and privileges*
champion**ship**	*the position or title of a winner*
fellow**ship**	*sharing similar interests or experiences, as by reason of profession, religion, or nationality*
hard**ship**	*extreme privation; suffering*

Put on your hard hat!

Think about it!
Use the four vocabulary words above to complete these sentences.

① My aunt has suffered from this _____ all of her life.

② Shelly was thrilled to hear that she received her United States _____.

③ Our extended family likes to _____ with one another.

④ The Dallas Cowboys won the _____.

Link colorful paperclips together in a loop to create a bracelet. Make a matching one for a friend!

Tack it on!

Name: _____

tion | state of, act of

celebra**tion**

Confetti and streamers fell from the air as the children enjoyed the birthday **celebration**.

Create a blueprint!

Draw it!
Add details to the illustration to show the meaning of the sentence.

Survey it!

Look it up!
Using a dictionary, write the definition of the word.

celebra**tion** – _____

_____

Saw through it!

Read each of the four words and their definitions.

vaca**tion**	*a period of time devoted to pleasure, rest, or relaxation*
tradi**tion**	*the passing down of elements of a culture from generation to generation, especially by oral communication*
participa**tion**	*the act of taking part or sharing in something*
opposi**tion**	*the act of opposing or resisting*

Put on your hard hat!

Think about it!

Use the four vocabulary words above to complete these sentences.

① There was much _____ between the two teams.

② Do not forget your camera when you go on _____.

③ The school fund raiser was a success! There was so much

_____.

④ It is a family _____ to have a big birthday dinner.

Create an imaginary party invitation. Be sure and think about who, what, where, when and why.

Tack it on!

Name: _____

y | inclined to, related to

dirt **y**

Create a blueprint!

Draw it!
Add details to the illustration to show the meaning of the sentence.

Outside of his house, the **dirty** pig played in the mud puddles.

Survey it!

Look it up!
Using a dictionary, write the definition of the word.

dirty – _____

_____

Saw through it!

Read each of the four words and their definitions.

sleepy	*ready for or needing sleep*
wealthy	*having an abundant supply of money or possessions of value*
whimsy	*an odd or fanciful idea; a whim*
furry	*covered with a dense coat of fine silky hairs*

Put on your hard hat!

Think about it!

Use the four vocabulary words above to complete these sentences.

① The llama was very _____.

② The baby was ready for her nap. She was _____.

③ The _____ man was generous and helped many needy people.

④ The fairy tale is full of _____.

Create a DIRT SURPRISE! Begin with chocolate pudding, add crushed Oreo® cookies on top, and finish off with a few gummy worms!

Tack it on!

Prefixes

Name: _____

Create a blueprint!

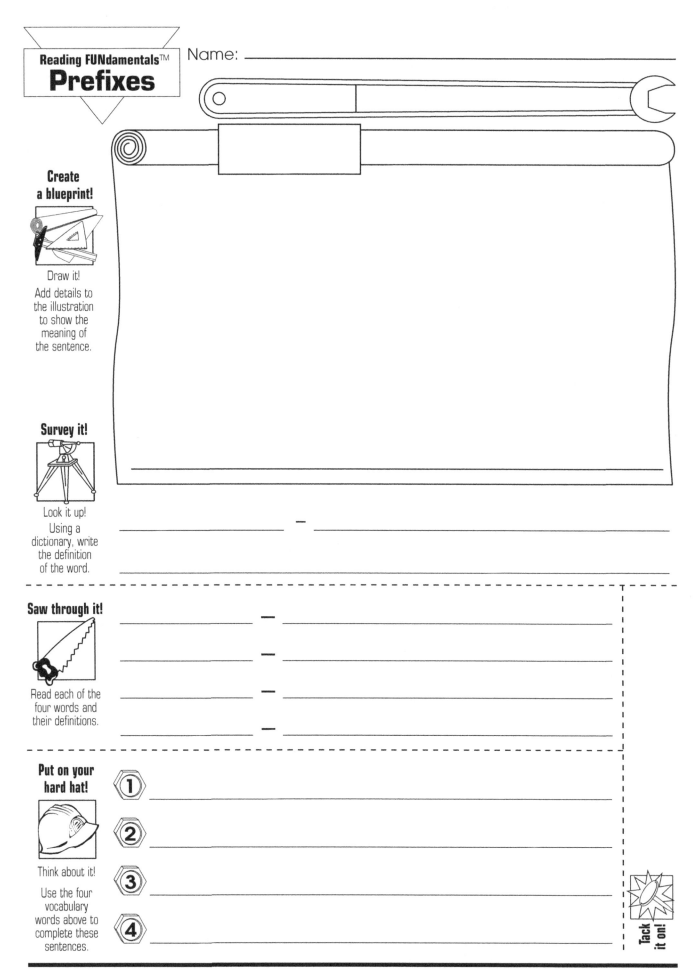

Draw it!
Add details to the illustration to show the meaning of the sentence.

Survey it!

Look it up!
Using a dictionary, write the definition of the word.

_____ — _____

_____

Saw through it!

Read each of the four words and their definitions.

Put on your hard hat!

Think about it!

Use the four vocabulary words above to complete these sentences.

① _____
② _____
③ _____
④ _____

Tack it on!

Name: _____

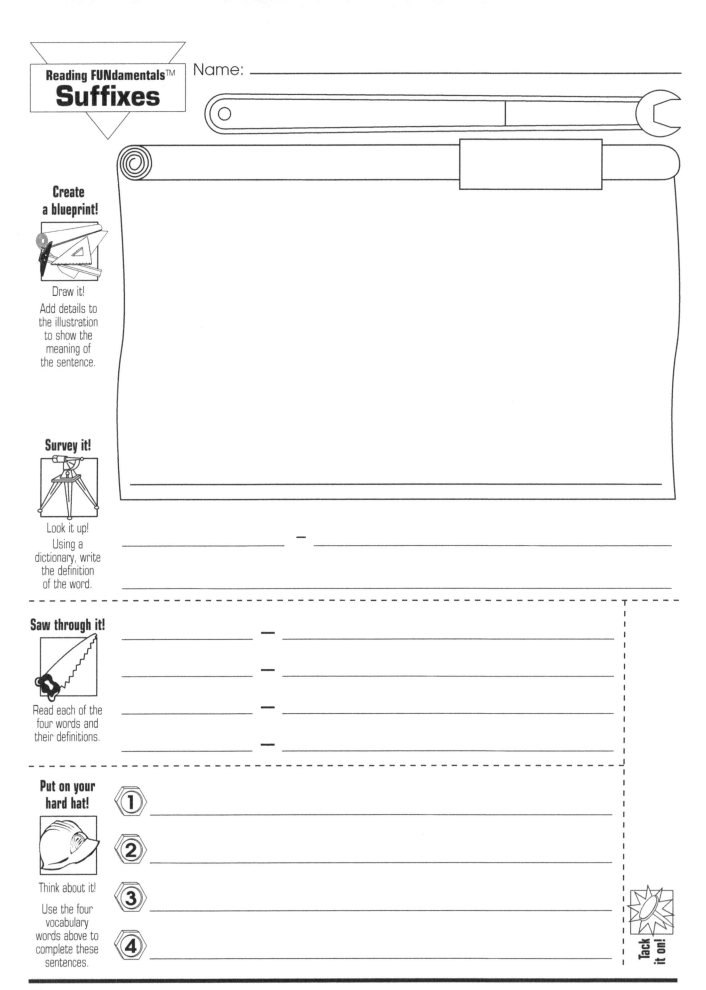

Create a blueprint!

Draw it!
Add details to the illustration to show the meaning of the sentence.

Survey it!

Look it up!
Using a dictionary, write the definition of the word.

_____ – _____

_____

Saw through it!

_____ – _____

_____ – _____

_____ – _____

_____ – _____

Read each of the four words and their definitions.

Put on your hard hat!

① _____

② _____

③ _____

④ _____

Think about it!

Use the four vocabulary words above to complete these sentences.

Tack it on!

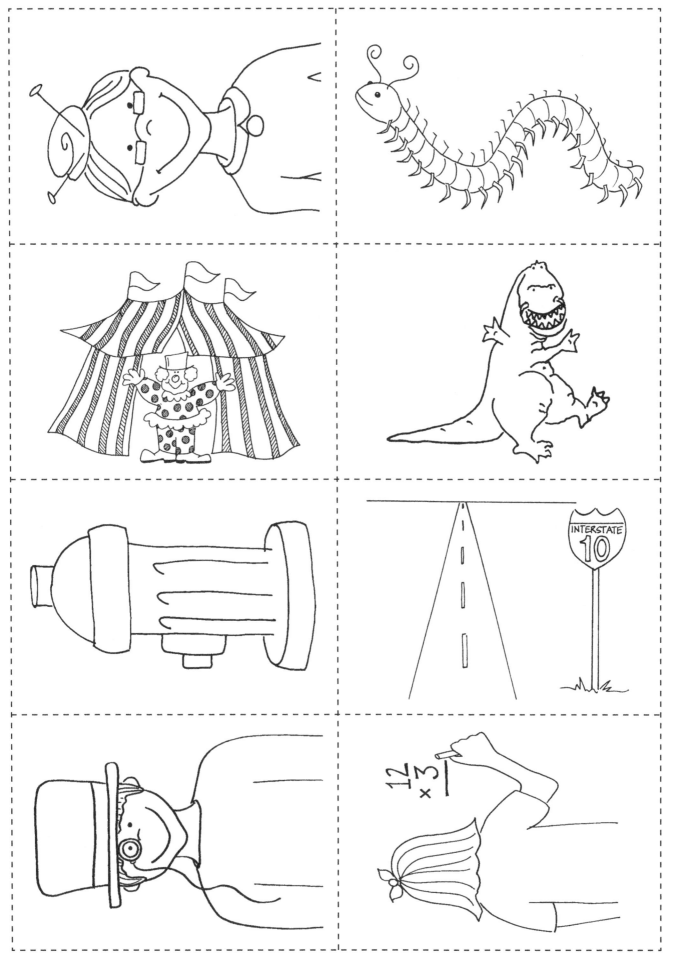